HAL•LEONARD
INSTRUMENTAL
PLAY-ALONG

AUDIO
ACCESS
INCLUDED

PLAYBACK+
Speed • Pitch • Balance • Loop

TRUMPET

PEACEFUL HYMNS

Audio arrangements by Peter Deneff

To access audio visit:
www.halleonard.com/mylibrary

Enter Code
3020-4057-5878-8315

T0057215

ISBN 978-1-70513-794-9

HAL•LEONARD®

Visit Hal Leonard Online at
www.halleonard.com

Contact us:
Hal Leonard
7777 West Bluemound Road
Milwaukee, WI 53213
Email: info@halleonard.com

In Europe, contact:
Hal Leonard Europe Limited
42 Wigmore Street
Marylebone, London, W1U 2RN
Email: info@halleonardeurope.com

In Australia, contact:
Hal Leonard Australia Pty. Ltd.
4 Lentara Court
Cheltenham, Victoria, 3192 Australia
Email: info@halleonard.com.au

ABIDE WITH ME

TRUMPET

Music by WILLIAM H. MONK

ALL CREATURES OF OUR GOD AND KING

TRUMPET

Music from *Geistliche Kirchengesang*

ALL HAIL THE POWER OF JESUS' NAME

TRUMPET

Music by OLIVER HOLDEN

ALL THROUGH THE NIGHT

TRUMPET

Welsh Folksong

AMAZING GRACE

TRUMPET

Traditional American Melody

BE THOU MY VISION

TRUMPET

Traditional Irish

Moderately slow

BLESSED ASSURANCE

TRUMPET

Music by PHOEBE PALMER KNAPP

COME, THOU FOUNT OF EVERY BLESSING

TRUMPET

Music from John Wyeth's *Repository of Sacred Music*

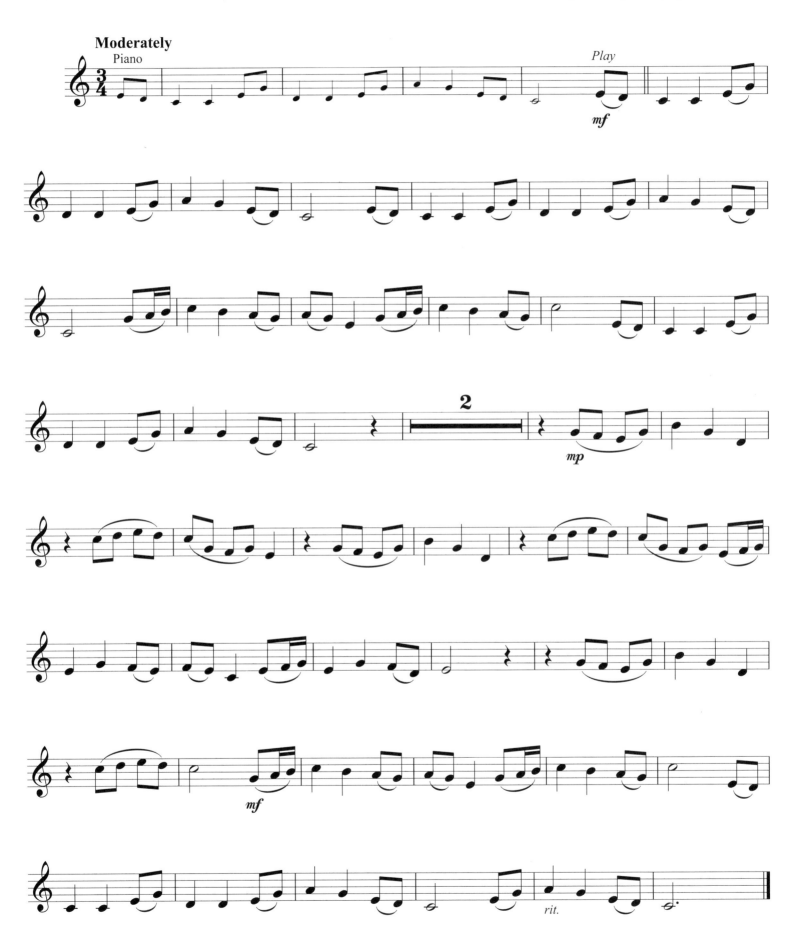

FAIREST LORD JESUS

TRUMPET

Music from *Schlesische Volkslieder*

FOR THE BEAUTY OF THE EARTH

TRUMPET

Music by CONRAD KOCHER

GREAT IS THY FAITHFULNESS

TRUMPET

Music by WILLIAM M. RUNYAN

Slowly, with feeling

HOLY, HOLY, HOLY

TRUMPET

Music by JOHN B. DYKES

HOW FIRM A FOUNDATION

TRUMPET

Traditional music compiled by JOSEPH FUNK

I NEED THEE EVERY HOUR

TRUMPET

Music by ROBERT LOWRY

IT IS WELL WITH MY SOUL

TRUMPET

Music by PHILIP P. BLISS

JUST AS I AM

TRUMPET

Music by WILLIAM B. BRADBURY

THE KING OF LOVE MY SHEPHERD IS

TRUMPET

Traditional Irish Melody

LET ALL MORTAL FLESH KEEP SILENCE

TRUMPET

17th Century French Carol

MY FAITH LOOKS UP TO THEE

TRUMPET

Music by LOWELL MASON

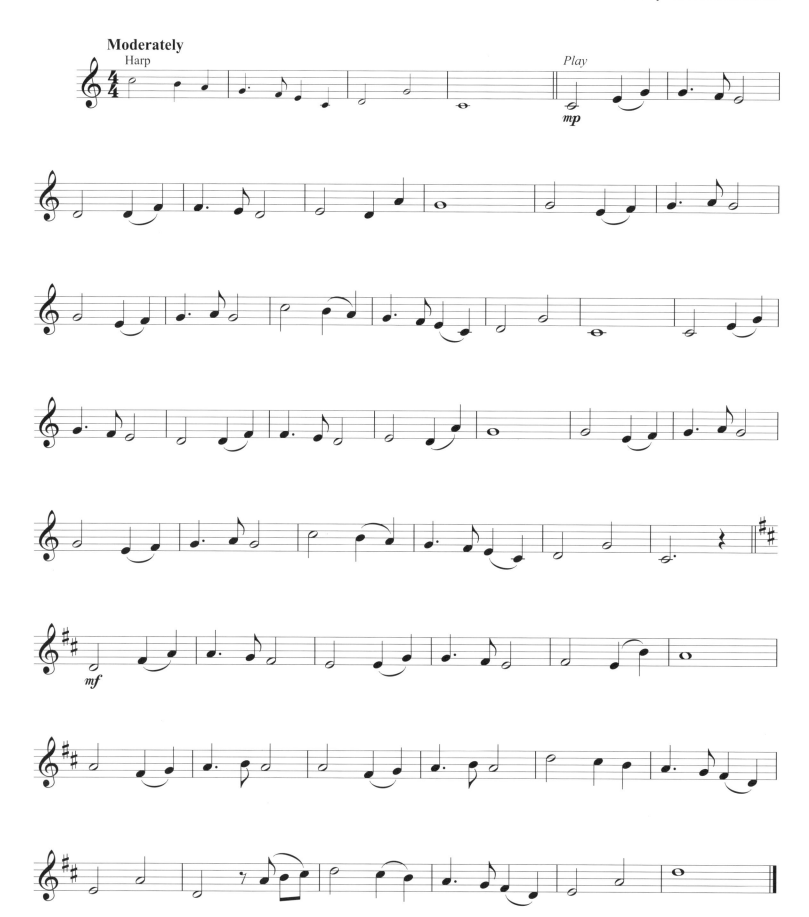

NEARER, MY GOD, TO THEE

TRUPMET

Music by LOWELL MASON

WERE YOU THERE WHEN THEY CRUCIFIED MY LORD?

TRUMPET

Traditional

WHAT A FRIEND WE HAVE IN JESUS

TRUMPET

Music by CHARLES C. CONVERSE

WONDROUS LOVE

TRUMPET

Southern American Folk Hymn